SUCCULENTS
OF SOUTHERN AFRICA
A FIRST FIELD GUIDE

Bead-leaved Vygie

Cape Speckled Aloe

JOHN MANNING

Contents

Silver Stoneflower

Struik Publishers
(a division of New Holland
Publishing (South Africa) (Pty) Ltd)
80 McKenzie Street
Cape Town 8001
South Africa
www.struik.co.za

First edition published in 2001

10 9 8 7 6 5 4 3 2 1

Publishing Manager: Pippa Parker
Managing Editor: Helen de Villiers
Editor: Mehita Iqani, Sally Woudberg
Designer: Dominic Robson

Reproduction: Scan Shop
Printing: CTP Book Printers

ISBN 1 86872 601 0

What are succulents?

Succulents are plants that have developed special water-storing tissue, which makes some part of the plant (the leaves, stem or roots) unusually fleshy or juicy. These moisture reserves evolved as a strategy for succulents to survive periods of drought or water stress. Drought can be caused by factors other than low rainfall in deserts, such as rock sheets that dry out quickly between rainfalls.

Succulents are not a group of related plants. Many plant types have developed fleshy water-storing tissue in order to endure drought. In southern Africa there are almost 30 plant families whose members are entirely, or partly, succulents.

Many people think that any strange-looking or prickly succulent is a type of cactus. Nothing could be further from the truth – although all cacti are succulent to a greater or lesser degree, they are just one of many different groups of succulent plants. True cacti are members of the Cactus Family, which are recognisable by showy flowers and fleshy fruits, and are indigenous[G] to the Americas. There is only one indigenous species of cactus in the whole of southern Africa – an inconspicuous trailing plant found on cliffs along the eastern seaboard of South Africa, which looks nothing like the well-known, rounded barrel cactus. All other cacti in southern Africa are originally from Central America, and have been introduced to the region, with disastrous results in some cases.

Scarlet Dew Flower

Succulent Karoo with tufted vygies

The remarkable similarity in appearance between some unrelated succulents demonstrates that environmental forces can have across-the-board effects on plant form. As the environment compels succulents to save water and reduce water loss, several natural laws of physics come into play. For instance, the more spherical an object, the smaller the ratio between its surface area and volume. This means that spherical bodies lose less water than flat objects. It is no surprise, then, that many succulents tend to have round, or globular leaves or stems. Other succulent characteristics that lessen water loss include a reduced leaf area; a thick, leathery epidermis[G] covered with a waxy layer; and the use of self-shading (protection from the sun of certain parts of the plant by its other parts). Another less obvious, but common strategy is the reduction of stomata[G] on the leaves and stem of the plant, and the concentration of these pores in deep grooves, where the evaporation rate is lower.

Types of succulents

Succulents store water in one or more of three main parts of the plant: the stems, leaves or roots. Leaf succulents concentrate the water-storing tissue in the leaves, which are thus quite fleshy, while the stems remain relatively slender. In stem succulents the primary water-storing tissue is located in the stems, which are juicy and succulent. The stems often become green and take over the photosynthetic^G function of the leaves. Many stem succulents thus have leaves that wither and fall off. In turn, the photosynthetic stem can become very leaf-like in appearance, and it is often difficult to distinguish true leaves from photosynthetic stems. Caudiciform succulents store water in swollen rootstocks^G or short stems at, or partly below, ground level. These storage organs produce short-lived, non-succulent, leafy shoots every growing season, which wither away during the subsequent dry season. The division between the three main types of succulence is not always absolute, and some plants may store water in more than one organ.

Where to find succulents

Succulents can be found in all climatic regions of the world, although most inhabit arid^G or semi-arid areas that experience seasonal climates. Southern Africa is exceptional in the wealth of its succulent flora. It is, in fact, home to more species of succulent, apart from cacti, than any other region of similar size in the world. Southern African succulents are particularly diverse. They range in size and habitat^G from miniature stoneplants, which are restricted to quartz pebble fields in Namaqualand; to giant candelabra trees that dominate thickets in the Eastern Cape; to forests of quiver trees in southern Namibia. Most southern African succulents, however, are small, difficult to find, and often sparsely distributed in isolated localities.

The most diverse concentration of succulents can be found in the appropriately named Succulent Karoo, in the south-western coastal area of South Africa. Unlike the rest of southern Africa, this region receives most of its rainfall during winter. It includes Namaqualand and the Little Karoo, both of which contain a large number of members of the Mesemb Family. For example, the Knersvlakte near Vanrhynsdorp, an arid[G] plain dominated by low chalk hillocks, red sandy flats, and extensive quartz pebble fields, has an abundance of beautiful dwarf mesembs, as well as stoneflowers and coneflowers. The Eastern Cape, by contrast, supports a wealth of succulents from the Aloe and Spurge families. It is home to more than 90% of all haworthias and more than three-quarters of the South African species of Euphorbia. The drier central regions of the sub-continent are also well endowed with succulents, especially members of the Milkweed Family. In the wetter, eastern parts of the region large numbers of succulents can be found in dry river valleys that run inland from the coast. Elsewhere in the region, succulents are often found inhabiting rocky outcrops or rock sheets, where the thin soil dries out rapidly.

Leaf-succulence is most common in the warm to temperate western parts of southern Africa, whereas stem-succulence becomes particularly prominent in the subtropical eastern parts of the sub-continent.

Conservation of succulents

A number of southern Africa's succulent species have become highly threatened – mainly due to industries, such as mining and agriculture. In some extreme cases, the known populations of several succulent species, including most of the haworthias, now consist of fewer than a hundred individuals.

Cushion Vygie

Fortunately, the majority of rare species that could be facing extinction, are in cultivation[G]. However, most succulents cannot easily be grown away from their natural habitats[G] without being given the appropriate care and attention. Plants should never be removed from the wild, and there is no need to do so since most species can be purchased from specialist nurseries.

Identifying succulents

Plants are classified by botanists into families largely according to the features of their flowers, which are often very distinctive. Characteristics such as the number of petals are useful: most succulents have flowers with five petals; the flowers of members of the Aloe Family always have six petals; while those of the Mesemb Family have numerous, very narrow petals. It is unfortunate, however, that many other useful features of the flowers are difficult to see, and that many succulents are only in flower for short periods of the year. It is not easy to identify succulents accurately when they are not in flower. There are a few exceptions, however. A useful characteristic for identifying members of the Spurge Family is that the stems ooze a milky latex[G] when damaged. This makes it easier to tell them apart from most similar-looking Milkweed succulents, which do not usually ooze a milky latex. (Non-succulent Milkweed plants, on the other hand, generally do.)

Most plant families develop only one of the three types of succulence discussed earlier. In this book, therefore, the plants are arranged within their families, according to types of succulence, starting with a single caudiciform succulent of the Yam Family. Leaf succulents from the Aloe and Mesemb Families come next, followed by members of the Daisy, Purslane and Stonecrop Families, which can develop either (or both) leaf and stem succulence. True stem succulents from the Grape, Geranium, Milkweed, Spurge and Cactus Families come last.

Explanations of words marked with a [G] appear on page 56.

Rock Vygie

8

Elephant's Foot

Dioscorea elephantipes

Yam Family

African names:
Olifantspoot (Afr)

Identification: Climbing perennials[G] with annual[G] stems, arising from a large, exposed, armour-plated tuber[G]. The spindly stems are twisted and warty[G], and bear heart-shaped leaves. The tiny greenish flowers have six petals. They are unisexual: the sexes appear on separate plants.

Succulent type: Root succulent.

Where found: Dry, rocky slopes.

Flowering time: March to May.

Notes: Popular among succulent enthusiasts, but increasingly rare in the wild. Plants are heavily grazed by goats. Tubers formed part of the traditional diet of local people. The twining[G] stems die off after fruiting and are replaced each year by new shoots. The seeds have a papery wing on one side that aids dispersal.

Status: Protected. Endemic[G].

Shrubby Bulbine

Bulbine frutescens

Aloe Family

African names:
Rankkopieva (Afr)

Identification: Clump-forming perennials[G] with creeping or sprawling stems that root along

their length. The pencil-shaped, succulent leaves are arranged in rosettes at the tips of branches. The yellow or orange flowers are carried in slender spikes above the leaves. They are star-shaped, about 10 mm in diameter, with six petals and six conspicuously bearded stamens[G] protruding from the centre.

Succulent type: Leaf succulent.

Where found: Rocky slopes in the arid[G] parts of the Western and Eastern Cape.

Flowering time: September to April.

Notes: Commonly grown in dry gardens and rockeries. Although each flower lasts less than a day, new buds open each day and the flower spike lengthens as it grows. Plants are easily propagated from cuttings.

Status: Not threatened. Endemic[G].

Cobweb Haworthia

Haworthia arachnoidea

Aloe Family

African names:
Spinnekop-
bolletjie (Afr)

Identification: Stemless
perennials[G] forming compact
rosettes up to 10 cm in diameter.
The tapering, succulent leaves are
arranged in tight rosettes, and are
covered on the margins and keel
with long, soft, white teeth. The
white flowers are about 15 mm
long and are carried on short,
often tilted spikes above the
leaves. They are tubular, with six
flaring petals.

Succulent type: Leaf succulent.

Where found: Rocky slopes,
usually under bushes.

Flowering time: November to
December.

Notes: An attractive pot-plant.
The long, wispy spines and the
dry, papery tips of the leaves
form a vegetable shade-cloth that
protects the plant from excessive
sunlight during the dry summer
months. For further protection,
the plants typically grow in the
shelter of small shrubs[G] or in
rock crevices.

Status: Not threatened.
Endemic[G].

Tongue-leaved Gasteria

Gasteria disticha

Aloe Family

African names:
Beestongblaar (Afr)

Identification: Stemless perennials[G] up to 20 cm high when not in flower. The oblong, succulent leaves are arranged opposite one another in flat fans, and are irregularly spotted with white. The surface and margins of the leaves are rough and sandpapery. The nodding flowers vary from pink to reddish, with greenish tips, and are carried in tilted, one-sided spikes that are up to 1 m high. The flowers are about 20 mm long and tubular and are conspicuously swollen at the base.

Succulent type: Leaf succulent.

Where found: Stony slopes and rocky hillsides in the shade of bushes.

Flowering time: July to October, rarely to February.

Notes: One of the earliest Cape plants to reach Europe, collected by the Dutch as early as 1689. The plants typically grow in the shelter of bushes, where they are protected from direct sunlight. Their speckled leaves provide an effective camouflage from predators. They are easily cultivated.

Status: Not threatened. Endemic[G].

Partridge Aloe

Aloe variegata

Aloe Family

African names:
Bontaalwyn,
Kanniedood (Afr),
Choje (San)

Identification: Stemless perennials[G] up to 25 cm high when not in flower. The sharply keeled leaves are arranged in three ranks and do not have spines or prickles. The thickened, white margins bear inconspicuous teeth, and the surface is attractively splashed or streaked with white. The relatively large flowers, about 30 mm long, are usually dull pink or red and are carried in short, often branched spikes above the leaves.

Succulent type: Leaf succulent.

Where found: Widespread on dry, stony flats in the arid[G] western interior of the country.

Flowering time: July to September.

Notes: One of the first aloes to be cultivated in Europe. It is a particularly attractive species with neat, boldly marked leaves and large flowers. In some parts of the Karoo it is grown on graves. Although very drought resistant, the plants are usually found in the shelter of small shrubs[G], which provide some protection against direct sunlight in the summer.

Status: Not threatened. Endemic[G].

Cape Speckled Aloe

Aloe microstigma

Aloe Family

Identification:
Rosette-forming perennials[G] up to 50 cm high when not in flower. The tapering, succulent leaves are often reddish, especially in the summer, and are usually covered with small, white spots. The margins bear sharp, reddish-brown teeth. The flowers are usually red in bud, but yellow when open, and are carried in conical spikes situated well above the leaves. They are tubular and 20–25 mm long.

Succulent type: Leaf succulent.

Where found: Stony slopes and amongst scrub[G] throughout the Little Karoo.

Flowering time: May to July.

Notes: Exceptionally common in the Little Karoo, dominating the rocky hillsides. The species is particularly conspicuous when in flower and is one of the floral highlights of the region in winter. It grows well in cultivation[G].

Status: Common. Endemic[G].

Krans Aloe

Aloe arborescens

Aloe Family

African names:
Kransaalwyn (Afr),
inHlazi (Zulu)

Identification: Many-branched shrubs[G] or small trees up to 2 m high, with stems often tilted. The sickle-shaped, succulent leaves are arranged in rosettes at the tips of the branches and bear sharp, greenish teeth along the margins. The flowers, which are about 30 mm long, range in colour from yellow through orange to pink or red, and are carried in short, conical spikes above the leaves.

Succulent type: Leaf succulent.

Where found: Widespread on rocky slopes and exposed ridges, typically in open scrub[G].

Flowering time: May to July.

Notes: A common and wide-spread species, often cultivated. Especially popular in the Eastern

Cape where it is used as a fence. It is widely grown throughout the world as an ornamental, and can be used as a convenient, natural first aid treatment for burns.

Status: Common.

Bitter Aloe

Aloe ferox

Aloe Family

African names:
Bitteraalwyn (Afr),
iKhala (Xhosa)

Identification: Robust, single-stemmed perennials[G] up to 5 m high, with old leaves remaining on the trunk. The tapering, succulent leaves are arranged in large rosettes at the top of the stem. The leaf margins, and sometimes the leaf surfaces, bear sharp, brown teeth. The flowers are usually orange to red, about 30 mm long and are carried in dense candelabras above the leaves. The flowers are tubular and bear petals, which curl upwards at the tips.

Succulent type: Leaf succulent.

Where found: Widely distributed on stony flats and slopes.

Flowering time: May to August, rarely to November.

Notes: One of the most widely distributed species of aloe, and the most important medicinal plant in the region. For over 200 years the golden-brown leaf sap has been used to make the purgative drug known as Cape Aloe. Overexploitation and careless harvesting pose a threat to the survival of the plants in some localities.

Status: Not threatened. Endemic[G].

Quiver Tree

Aloe dichotoma

Aloe Family

African names:
Kokerboom (Afr),
Choje (San)

Identification: Sturdy trees up to 9 m high, with rounded crowns. The thick trunks are covered with smooth bark that fragments into large, golden-brown scales. The tapering, succulent leaves are arranged in rosettes at the tips of the branches, and bear inconspicuous teeth along the margins. The flowers are carried in short spikes among the leaves, and are about 30 mm long. They are yellow and narrowly urn-shaped, with six petals and six reddish stamens[G] that protrude from the narrow mouth.

Succulent type: Leaf and stem succulent.

Where found: Rocky slopes in the arid[G] parts of southern Namibia, Namaqualand and Bushmanland.

Flowering time: June to August.

Notes: One of the few truly tree-like aloes. Its hollow branches were used as quivers by the San. It is widely cultivated in the Northern Cape, adorning grave-yards, school grounds and farm-yards. Near Nieuwoudtville the plants grow in thousands, forming the famous Quiver Tree forests.

Status: Not threatened. Endemic[G].

Ice Plant

Mesembryanthemum guerichianum

Mesemb Family

African names:
Brakslaai (Afr);
Kama, Nuta (Koi)

Identification: Sprawling annual^G herbs with smooth, angled stems and succulent leaves covered with glistening water cells. The young leaves are in a basal^G rosette, but later become scattered along the stems. They are flat, broad, soft and very juicy. The daisy-like flowers are carried in clusters and are 25–30 mm in diameter. The numerous thread-like petals are white or pinkish, and grade into the stamens^G. The numerous stamens are clustered in a central hollow. The fruits are five-sided.

Succulent type: Leaf succulent.

Where found: Widely distributed throughout the dry western parts of southern Africa, on sandy flats and roadsides.

Flowering time: August to December.

Notes: These somewhat weed-like plants are usually found in places that have been disturbed, such as overgrazed rangelands, roadsides and river margins. They grow easily from seed. Flowers open only on warm, sunny days, and close in the evening.

Status: Not threatened. Endemic^G.

Silver Stoneflower

Argyroderma delaetii

Mesemb Family

African names:
Bababoudjies,
Jakkalsniertjie (Afr)

Identification: Dwarf succulents
up to 5 cm high, solitary or clustered together in clumps. The
leaves are reduced to a single
pair, and are almost globular,
smooth, silver-skinned, firm
and highly succulent. The daisy-like flowers are produced from
between the leaves and are
30–40 mm in diameter. The
numerous narrow petals are white
to purple or yellow. The fruits are
14–18 sided.

Succulent type: Leaf
succulent.

Where found:
Confined to quartz
patches on the arid[G]
flats known as the
Knersvlakte, just
north of
Vanrhynsdorp.

Flowering time: April to June.

Notes: During the dry summer
months the leaves shrink, drawing
the plants down amongst the
surrounding quartz pebbles,
where they receive some protection from the sun. The withered
remains of old leaves form a
protective skin over the
replacement pair. Extremely
popular among collectors. They
should be watered sparingly,
otherwise the leaves may burst
from too much water.

Status: Locally common.
Endemic[G].

Coneflower

Conophytum minutum

Mesemb Family

African names:
Toontjies (Afr)

Identification: Dwarf succulents up to 5 cm high, forming clumps. Leaves are reduced to a single pair that are joined together and separated at the top by a small mouth-like slit. Body is cone-shaped, firm and highly succulent. Daisy-like flowers are produced from the slit at the top of the plant body and are 10–15 mm in diameter. Numerous narrow petals are pink to purple or occasionally white, and joined below by a long, narrow tube. Fruits are 4–5 sided.

Succulent type: Leaf succulent.

Where found: Southern Namaqualand, stony outcrops or gravel patches.

Flowering time: March to May.

Notes: Among the most charming and curious of the various stoneplants. The withered remains of the old leaves form a protective skin over the replacement pair, which burst out at the start of the next growing season. Coneflowers are extremely popular, and have been almost exterminated in the wild by avaricious and unscrupulous collectors. They differ from stoneflowers in that they are winter-growing, and the flower's petals are joined together at the bottom to form a tube.

Status: Locally common. Endemic[G].

toneplant

ithops ruschiorum

Mesemb Family

African names:
Beeskloutjie (Afr)

dentification: Dwarf succulents
ip to 5 cm high, usually forming
clumps. The leaves are reduced to
a single pair that are joined
together for most of their length,
lattened on top and separated by
a slit. The body is cone-shaped,
irm and highly succulent, and
he tops of the leaves are beau-
ifully mottled. The daisy-like
lowers are produced from the
gap between the leaves and are
20–25 mm in diameter. Numerous narrow petals are bright
vellow. The numerous stamens[G]
are clustered in the centre. The
ruits are five-sided.

Succulent type: Leaf succulent.

Where found: On gravelly
patches along the coast of
southern Namibia.

Flowering time: July to August.

Notes: Very difficult to detect
in the wild when not in flower.
Most of the plant body is buried
and only the tops of the leaves
protrude above the surface. Well-
camouflaged by their mottled
markings, which often match the
colours of the surrounding
pebbles. Each pair of leaves lasts
only a single season, and the
withered remains of the old
leaves form a protective skin
around the replacement pair,
which burst out at the start of
the next growing season. Stoneplants are widely cultivated by
succulent specialists throughout
the world.

Status: Local. Endemic[G].

Showy Lampranthus

Lampranthus amoenus

Mesemb Family

African names:
Vygie (Afr)

Identification: Rounded shrublets^G up to 1 m high, with smooth stems and leaves. The leaves are scattered along the stems in pairs. They are cylindrical or slightly triangular, firm and succulent. The daisy-like flowers are carried in threes and are 30–40 mm in diameter.

The numerous narrow petals are usually brilliant purple and occasionally white. The fruits are five-sided.

Succulent type: Leaf succulent.

Where found: Restricted to sandy flats along the West Coast in the Cape.

Flowering time: September to October.

Notes: Densely covered with brilliant purple flowers in the spring. The flowers open only on warm, sunny days and close in the evening. A popular rockery plant in South African gardens.

Status: Not threatened. Endemic^G.

Collared Ruschia

Ruschia tecta

Mesemb Family

African names:
Beesvygie (Afr)

Identification: Erect shrublets^G up to 1 m high, with smooth stems and leaves. The leaves are scattered along the stems in pairs, and are joined at the base to form slightly swollen collars around the stems. They are almost cylindrical and slightly S-shaped, and are firm and succulent. The daisy-like flowers occur in dense, flat-topped clusters and are about 30 mm in diameter. The numerous narrow petals are purple, becoming whitish towards the base, forming a pale halo. The fruits are six-sided.

Succulent type: Leaf succulent.

Where found: Restricted to sandy coastal flats along the West Coast in the Western Cape.

Flowering time: September to October.

Notes: A rather untidy shrub. The flowers open only on warm, sunny days and close in the evenings. A hardy plant, suited to cultivation^G.

Status: Not threatened. Endemic^G.

Scarlet Dew Flower

Drosanthemum speciosum

Mesemb Family

African names:
Rooi Douvygie
(Afr)

Identification: Twiggy shrublets^G up to 60 cm in height, with short hairs on young stems and prominent glistening water cells on young leaves. The short-lived leaves are scattered in pairs along the stems and drop easily. They are cylindrical, blunt, soft and succulent. The daisy-like flowers are 30–40 mm in diameter and are carried in small clusters. The numerous narrow petals range in colour from orange to red, but are always whitish towards the base, forming a pale halo. Innermost petals are small and black. The fruits are five-sided.

Succulent type:
Leaf succulent.

Where found: Restricted to dry shale hillsides in the western Little Karoo.

Flowering time: September to November.

Notes: Usually occur in colonies, and are spectacular when in flower. The flowers open only on warm, sunny days and close in the evenings. A popular plant, found in Mediterranean gardens throughout the world.

Status: Not threatened. Endemic^G.

Sour Fig

Carpobrotus edulis

Mesemb Family

African names:
Suurvy (Afr),
Gaukum (Koi)

Identification: Robust perennial[G] herbs with smooth, trailing stems up to 2 m long. The wedge-like leaves are very succulent and are scattered in pairs along the stems. The large, daisy-like flowers are carried singly on short stalks and are 80–100 mm in diameter. The numerous narrow petals are pale yellow when fresh, but turn pink with age. Fruits are fleshy when green, but gradually dry out. Seeds are contained in a slimy pulp.

Succulent type: Leaf succulent.

Where found: Widely distributed in the winter rainfall region as well as the Eastern Cape, especially along the coast. It is naturalised in many parts of the world, particularly regions with winter rains and hot dry summers, such as Australia and California.

Flowering time: August to October.

Notes: Occur in dense mats, often along roadsides. Plants grow easily from cuttings and are commonly cultivated in coastal gardens. They are used extensively in landscaping attempts to stabilise sandy banks and road verges. The dried fruits have a pleasant, sour taste and are widely eaten in the Western Cape. They are used to make 'Suurvy' jam.

Status: Not threatened. Endemic[G].

Buckbay Vygie

Dorotheanthus bellidiformis

Mesemb Family

African names:
Bokbaaivygie,
Sandvygie (Afr)

Identification: Dwarf annual[G]
herbs up to 10 cm high, with
prominent, glistening water cells
on the leaves and stems. The
leaves are oblong, but taper
sharply towards the base, and are
soft and succulent. The daisy-like
flowers are 20–30 mm in
diameter and are carried singly
on slender, leafless stalks. The
numerous narrow petals vary in
colour from white to pink,
yellow or orange, and are
often lighter towards the base,
forming a pale halo. The fruits
are five-sided.

Succulent type: Annual[G] leaf
succulent.

Where found: Widely distributed
in the winter rainfall region,
especially along the coast; mostly
on sandy flats.

Flowering time: August to
September.

Notes: Often occur in large
colonies. Flowers are very
variable in colour; open only on
warm, sunny days and close in
the evenings. A well-known
garden plant, widely cultivated in
many parts of the world.

Status: Not threatened.
Endemic[G].

Baboon's Toes

Senecio radicans

Daisy Family

African names: Bobbejaan-toontjies (Afr)

Identification: Trailing perennials[G] with slender stems. The leaves are often arranged in a single, upright row along the top of the creeping stems and are spindle-shaped and very succulent. They have a transparent, strip-like window along the upper side. The fragrant flower heads are white or mauve, without petal-like outer florets[G], about 5 mm long, and carried on slender, upright stalks.

Succulent type: Leaf succulent.

Where found: Trailing on exposed rock outcrops.

Flowering time: April to September.

Notes: Leaves swell and turn green when wet, exposing the transparent window through which light can enter the leaf for photosynthesis[G]. Under conditions of drought the leaves turn red and crease along the window, thereby preventing light from entering. This interesting plant is well known to specialist succulent growers.

Status: Not threatened. Endemic[G].

Sjambokbush

Kleinia longiflora

Daisy Family

African names:
Sambokbossie (Afr)

Identification: Spindly shrublets[G] with ridged, cylindrical succulent stems. The leaves are very small or non-existent. The flower heads are very slender and are scattered along the stems. Flowerheads are white to yellowish, without petal-like outer florets[G], and about 20 mm long.

Succulent type: Stem succulent.

Where found: Dry, rocky slopes.

Flowering time: March to May.

Notes: An unusual plant that somewhat resembles a species of Euphorbia in its naked, cylindrical stems. The seeds are equipped with a conspicuous feathery parachute that aids in dispersal.

Status: Not threatened. Endemic[G].

Coral Senecio

Kleinia fulgens

Daisy Family

Identification:
Perennial^G herbs with erect or sprawling succulent stems, projecting from a tuber^G-like root. The leathery, fleshy leaves are narrow towards the base and toothed along the margin. The flower-heads are carried singly on long stalks above the leaves. Flowerheads are orange to red, without petal-like outer florets^G, and about 25 mm in diameter.

Succulent type: Stem and leaf succulent.

Where found: Steep, rocky slopes and cliffs.

Flowering time: January to August.

Notes: Attractive, hardy garden plant. The seeds are equipped with feathery parachutes that aid in dispersal.

Status: Not threatened.

Elephant Bush

Portulacaria afra

Purslane Family

African names:
Spekboom (Afr)

Identification: Succulent shrubs^G
or small trees up to 3 m high,
with smooth, jointed branches
and swollen stems. The leathery,
rounded leaves are in opposite
pairs. The small, star-shaped
flowers, about 5 mm in diameter,
are carried in dense spikes that
are crowded at the branch tips.
They are pink to purplish, with
five pointed petals.

Succulent type: Stem and leaf
succulent.

Where found: Rocky hillsides in
dry scrub^G.

Flowering time: October to
November.

Notes: Widely planted as a hedge
as it is quick-growing, hardy,
and evergreen. It is also used to
prevent soil erosion, as the roots
bind the soil effectively. The
plant is a valuable fodder for
many browsing animals. The
dried, powdered leaves can be
used to make snuff.

Status: Not threatened.
Endemic^G.

Red Treasure

Crassula perfoliata

Stonecrop Family

African names:
Rooiplakkie (Afr)

Identification: Erect perennials^G up to 1 m high, with stems and leaves that are covered with tiny, rounded warts^G. The stiff, succulent leaves occur in pairs, and vary in shape from narrow and lance-like to rather broad and blunt. The small, shallow, urn-shaped flowers are 6–12 mm in diameter, with five petals, and are carried in flat-topped clusters at the tips of the stems. Plants from the Eastern Cape have pink to brilliant red flowers, but further north the flowers tend to be whiter in colour.

Succulent type: Leaf succulent.

Where found: Rocky grassland or scrub^G in river valleys and ravines.

Flowering time: November to February.

Notes: The red-flowered variety was introduced into cultivation^G in Europe in the late 1700s, and has become a highly popular container plant.

Status: Not threatened. Endemic^G.

Scentbottle

Crassula columnaris

Stonecrop Family

African names:
Koesnaatjie (Afr)

Identification: Dwarf
perennials[G] or biennials[G] up to
10 cm high. The stems are
covered by closely overlapping
leaves and usually have small
branches at the base. The
succulent leaves are positioned in
opposite pairs and resemble
lumps of plasticine that have
been pressed together. The
narrow, urn-shaped flowers are
highly scented and are crowded
in a round, head-like cluster at
the tip of the stem. Flowers vary
in colour from white to yellow,
and are sometimes tinged with
red. About 5 mm in diameter,
with five petals.

Succulent type: Leaf succulent.

Where found: In depressions or
gentle slopes, often among quartz
pebbles or, less commonly, in
rock crevices.

Flowering time: May to August.

Notes: The stem of this charming
succulent dies each year after
flowering and seed set. Plants
from Namaqualand and southern
Namibia produce small branches
at the base of the main stem that
continue to flower in the follow-
ing season, but plants from the
Little Karoo have to reproduce by
seed each season. These plants
are biennial, so it is necessary to
grow them from seed each year
as they cannot be transplanted.

Status: Not threatened.
Endemic[G].

Dog's Ears

Cotyledon orbiculata

Stonecrop Family

African names: Kouterie (Afr)

Identification: Sprawling shrublets[G] up to 1 m high, covered with a thin, whitish bloom. The succulent leaves vary from cigar to paddle-shaped, and are arranged in pairs or whorls[G]. Leaves are thick and usually smooth in texture, although

sometimes covered with velvety hairs. The reddish to yellow flowers are carried in clusters at the ends of tall stems, well above the leaves. They are urn-shaped, with slightly swollen bases and five petals that curl back at the ends. Flowers are 20–30 mm long and nod conspicuously. Flower stalks straighten when in fruit, and the fruits are held upright.

Succulent type: Leaf succulent.

Where found: Rocky or stony slopes in scrub[G].

Flowering time: October to January.

Notes: A commonly cultivated plant. Nectar from the flowers is very sought-after by sunbirds. The leaf pulp can be used in the treatment of warts[G], and as a poultice for boils and abscesses.

Status: Not threatened. Endemic[G].

White Lady

Kalanchoe thyrsiflora

Stonecrop Family

African names:
Geelplakkie (Afr),
uTywala Bentaka
(Xhosa), uTshwala
Benyoni (Zulu)

Identification: Robust
perennials[G] up to 1.5 m high,
covered with a silvery bloom.

The succulent, paddle-shaped
leaves are arranged in a basal[G]
rosette and are often flushed
reddish. The narrow, urn-shaped
flowers are tightly clustered in a
cylindrical spike. The sweetly
scented flowers have greenish
tubes, 15–20 mm long, and five
brilliant yellow petals.

Succulent type: Leaf succulent.

Where found: Rocky outcrops
situated on hills in grassland and
bushveld.

Flowering time: February to
September.

Notes: The leaf rosettes produce
a flowering stem in their second
year, after which they die. The
plant subsequently resprouts
from the rootstock[G]. A popular
garden plant. Traditionally used
to treat earache, colds and
intestinal worms.

Status: Not threatened.
Endemic[G].

Kalanchoe

Kalanchoe rotundifolia

Stonecrop Family

African names: Nentabos (Afr), mFayisele Yasehlatini (Xhosa), uChane (Zulu)

Identification: Slender, sometimes straggling, perennials^G up to 1.2 m high, often found in colonies. The leathery leaves are in opposite pairs and vary greatly in shape from smooth and round to toothed, scalloped or even three-lobed^G. The narrow, urn-shaped flowers are borne in several small clusters on slender stalks. The flowers range from orange to red, and have slender 5–15 mm long tubes, which are swollen at the base. Each tube bears four narrow petals.

Succulent type: Leaf succulent.

Where found: Usually in shade or half-shade, often in dense stands under trees or shrubs^G in bushveld.

Flowering time: March to December.

Notes: Widespread, often grown in rockeries. Poisonous to stock. Has been used as an emetic.

Status: Not threatened. Endemic^G.

Butterbush

Tylecodon paniculatus

Stonecrop Family

African names:
Botterboom (Afr)

Identification: Shrublets[G] up to 1.5 m high, with smooth, swollen stems covered with yellowish peeling bark. The succulent, paddle-shaped leaves are deciduous[G], and fall or dry out before the plant flowers. The reddish, nodding flowers are carried on branched stems. The flowers are urn-shaped, with five petals that curl back at the ends, and are 20–30 mm long.

Succulent type: Stem and leaf succulent.

Where found: Rocky or stony slopes in scrub[G].

Flowering time: November to December.

Notes: Common on low, stony hillsides in the Western Cape and Namaqualand. The flowers are visited by sunbirds for nectar.

Status: Not threatened. Endemic[G].

ellow Butterbush

ylecodon wallichii

Stonecrop Family

African names:
Geel Botterboom
(Afr)

dentification: Shrublets[G] up to
m high, with thick, warty[G]
ems. The lance-shaped,
succulent leaves are deciduous[G],
nd fall by flowering time. The
ellow or greenish-yellow
owers are carried on branched
ems and are urn-shaped, with

five petals that curl back at the
ends. They are 15–20 mm long.

Succulent type: Stem and leaf
succulent.

Where found: Sandy or gravelly
slopes.

Flowering time: December to
February.

Status: Not threatened.
Endemic[G].

Baines' Cyphostemma

Cyphostemma bainesii

Grape Family

Identification:
Robust shrublets[G]
up to 1 m high, with
thick, swollen stems arising from
a large tuber[G]-like rootstock[G]. The
bark is papery and dull white.
The leaves are crowded at the
ends of the branches on very
short stalks. Each leaf is divided
into three smooth, leathery
leaflets that are evenly toothed
along the margins. The small,
greenish-yellow flowers, with
five petals each, are carried in
flat-topped clusters at the branch
tips, just before the leaves. Juicy
red berries appear after flowering.

Succulent type: Stem succulent.

Where found: Stony granite
hillsides.

Flowering time: November to
January.

Notes: A curious-
looking shrub that
resembles a very
small baobab tree.
It is commonly
found on the granite
hills surrounding
Windhoek, where
it was first
documented by
the artist and
explorer, Thomas
Baines, in 1861.

Status: Protected.
Endemic[G].

Vineskin Cyphostemma

Cyphostemma uter

Grape Family

Identification:
Robust shrubs^G up to 1.5 m high, with thick, swollen stems arising from a large, tuber^G-like rootstock^G. The bark is papery and dull white. The leaves are crowded together at the ends of branches. Each leaf is divided into five coarsely-toothed leaflets, which are covered with glandular hairs. Small greenish-yellow flowers have five petals each, and are carried in flat-topped clusters at the branch tips, next to the leaves. Juicy red berries appear after flowering.

Succulent type:
Stem succulent.

Where found:
Grows only in deep valleys running into the Cunene River, on the Namibia/Angola border. Favours east-facing, dry, stony slopes.

Flowering time: September to October.

Notes: A remarkable shrub that resembles a small baobab tree. Early explorers likened the swollen trunk to animal skins used for storing wine or water.

Status: Protected.

Common Candlebush

Monsonia crassicaule

Geranium Family

African names: Kaiingbos, Boesmanskers (Afr), Noerap (San)

Identification: Spiny shrublets[G] up to 50 cm high, with fleshy stems. The leaves form tufts[G] at the base of long, deciduous[G] spines that are scattered on the stems. Leaf blades are triangular, with coarse teeth on the margins. The large, creamy white flowers are about 40–50 mm in diameter and are carried on stalks among the leaves. Flowers are bowl-shaped, with five highly creased petals, and fifteen stamens[G] clustered in the centre.

Succulent type: Stem succulent.

Where found: Dry, rocky and stony slopes.

Flowering time: May to June.

Notes: An important source of fuel to early settlers as their waxy bark causes them to burn

readily. The spines are formed from the dry leaf stalks, and discourage browsing animals. The leaf blades are short-lived, but the stems' ability to photosynthese[G] enables the plants to live without leaves during periods of prolonged drought.

Status: Not threatened. Endemic[G].

Prickly Pelargonium

Pelargonium crithmifolium

Geranium Family

African names:
Dikbasmalva (Afr)

Identification: Shrublets[G] up to 70 cm high, with thick, knobbly stems. The deciduous[G] leaves are crowded near the ends of the branches. The leaf blades are divided into narrow, slightly fleshy lobes[G]. The white flowers are marked with red at the base of the upper petals, and are carried on highly branched stalks among the leaves. Flowers are about 15 mm in diameter and star-shaped, with five very narrow petals and five stamens[G] clustered in the centre.

Succulent type: Stem succulent.

Where found: Dry, rocky and stony slopes, sometimes in rock crevices.

Flowering time: May to October.

Notes: The flower stalks become hard and thorny after flowering, and form a shield over the plant that protects it from herbivores and the hot summer sun. The needle-like fruits split lengthways into five narrow strips that roll up to release the seeds. Each seed has a plume-like parachute, which is used during dispersal.

Status: Not threatened. Endemic[G].

Impala Lily

Adenium multiflorum

Milkweed Family

African names:
Impalalelie (Afr),
isiGubenguba (Zulu)

Identification: Shrubs[G] up to 3 m high, with thick, swollen stems arising from large, tuber[G]-like rootstocks[G]. The deciduous[G] leaves are clustered at the ends of the branches and appear only after flowering. The leaf blades are slightly fleshy or leathery. Flowers are showy, about 50 mm in diameter; white to pale pink, with dark pink margins. Flowers are tube-like beneath five spread-out petals. Stamens[G] are hidden in the tubes.

Succulent type: Stem succulent.

Where found: Rocky or stony slopes of dry lowland woodlands.

Flowering time: May to September.

Notes: Lovely garden or container plant, best grown from seed in frost-free areas. The exotic flowers are produced in the winter months before the leaves appear. The paired, cigar-shaped fruits split to release the rod-like seeds, which are equipped with tufts[G] of hairs at each end for dispersal. All parts of the plant are heavily grazed by game and stock.

Status: Not threatened.

Halfmens

Pachypodium namaquanum

Milkweed Family

Identification:
Small trees up to
3 m high. Tapering,
swollen stems, usually without
branches and covered with spine-
tipped warts^G. Deciduous^G,
velvety leaves are clustered
together at the tip of the stem.
The flowers are about 50 mm
long, yellowish-green on the
outside and red on the inside.
They are tube-like, with five
short petals. The stamens^G are
hidden in the tube.

Succulent type: Stem succulent.

Where found: Very arid^G, rocky
slopes in the Richtersveld and
southern Namibia.

Flowering time: July to
September.

Notes: Stems always tilt towards
the north, probably to guard
against overheating in summer.
The bizarre, almost human

appearance and tendency to lean
northwards inspired the San
legend that the plants represent
tribal ancestors gazing
nostalgically towards their former
homes in the Kalahari. The plants
do not thrive away from their
natural desert environment.

Status: Protected. Endemic^G.

Hoodia

Hoodia gordonii

Milkweed Family

African names:
Wolweghaap (Afr)

Identification: Robust, leafless succulents with clumps of 11–17 sided stems that are covered with spine-tipped warts[G]. Flowers vary in length from 40–100 mm and are produced near the top of the stems. They are saucer-shaped, with five short petals that are curled out of sight beneath the rim; they range in colour from pink to maroon, and are somewhat foul-smelling.

Succulent type: Stem succulent.

Where found: Dry, stony slopes and flats.

Flowering time: September to April.

Notes: A spectacular plant that was first collected in 1779 by Sir Robert Gordon, who was an explorer and Commander of the Garrison at the Cape, during his trip to chart the mouth of the Orange (now Gariep) River.

Status: Protected. Endemic[G].

Devil's Trumpet

Tavaresia barklyi

Milkweed Family

Identification:
Leafless succulents with clumps of 10–12 sided stems that have corners covered with white warts[G], tipped with three white or purple bristles. The flowers vary in length from 40–110 mm, and are produced near the base of the young stems. They are tube- or trumpet-shaped. They bear five short petals that are pale yellow with purple spots; purple at the base of the tube, and warty on the inside.

Succulent type: Stem succulent.

Where found: Rocky hillsides in dry scrub[G].

Flowering time: November to April.

Notes: This striking and interesting species derives its Latin name from Sir Henry Barkly, who was Governor of the Cape from 1870 to 1877, and who collected and documented the species in 1871.

Status: Not threatened.

Giant Carrion Flower

Stapelia gigantea

Milkweed Family

African names:
Grootaasblom (Afr),
iLilo eLikhulu,
isiHlelhe (Zulu).

Identification: Leafless succulents with short, creeping stems that form mats up to 50 cm in diameter. The stems are velvety and four-sided, with rows of small warts[G] along each corner. The large flowers, 125–400 mm in diameter, are produced singly near the base of the stems and rest on the ground. They are leathery and wrinkled; covered with long, shaggy hairs. The five tapering petals are yellow to pink, with reddish wrinkles. The flowers smell very strongly of rotten meat.

Succulent type:
Stem succulent.

Where found: Rocky hillsides in dry scrub[G].

Flowering time: March to May.

Notes: One of the largest flowers in the plant kingdom. The foul-smelling flowers are pollinated by carrion flies that are deceived into thinking that they have come upon a suitable carcass on which to lay their eggs. The plant has several traditional medicinal uses, also allegedly used as a poison by sorcerers.

Status: Not threatened.

Cape Carrion Flower

Orbea variegata

Milkweed Family

African names:
Aasblom (Afr).

Identification: Leafless succulents with short, creeping stems that intertwine to form mats up to 50 cm in diameter. The stems bear four rows of conical warts[G]. The flowers are large; 70–110 mm in diameter. They are produced singly, near the base of the stems, and rest on the surface. They are leathery and wrinkled, with five spreading petals that are cream to yellow, and spotted or mottled with brown. In the centre of each flower is a conspicuously raised ring. The flowers have a characteristically unpleasant smell.

Succulent type: Stem succulent.

Where found: Rocky outcrops, usually near the coast.

Flowering time: December to September.

Notes: Well-known around Cape Town. Although the flowers are large, they are not easy to spot. Despite this, they did not escape the attention of early Dutch sailors, and the plant became one of the first South African species to be transported alive to Europe, in 1624.

Status: Not threatened. Endemic[G].

Yellow Carrion Flower

Orbeopsis lutea

Milkweed Family

African names: Geelaasblom, Slangghaap (Afr).

Identification: Leafless succulents with short, creeping stems that form mats up to 50 cm in diameter. The stems are four-sided, with rows of sharp, conical teeth along the corners, and are sometimes mottled with purple. The flowers are 40–70 mm in diameter and are produced in clusters near the base of the stems. They are leathery and wrinkled, with five tapering petals that are yellow (or reddish in Namibia) with vibrating, club-shaped purple hairs along the margins. The flowers smell very strongly of rotten fish.

Succulent type: Stem succulent.

Where found: Rocky outcrops in scrub[G].

Flowering time: January to April.

Notes: One of the most noxious, yet brilliant, of the carrion flowers. Its foul-smelling flowers attract the attention of carrion flies, which unwittingly pollinate the flowers when successfully deceived into laying eggs on them.

Status: Not threatened.

Striped Carrion Flower

Huernia zebrina

Milkweed Family

Identification:
Leafless succulents with short, creeping stems that form mats of up to 30 cm in diameter. The stems are five-sided, with rows of sharp teeth along the corners. The star-shaped flowers are produced near the base of the stems and are 30–50 mm in diameter. Flowers have a conspicuous, glossy ring in the centre, and have five spreading petals that are pale yellow with bold, brown stripes. Flowers have an unpleasant scent.

Succulent type:
Stem succulent.

Where found:
Stony slopes and flats in lowland scrub^G, typically under bushes.

Flowering time: February to July.

Notes: This is a very attractive species that responds well to careful cultivation^G. The glossy ring in the flower's centre, which looks a little like a life buoy, is a characteristic of several related species.

Status: Not threatened. Endemic^G.

Vegetable Football

Euphorbia obesa

Spurge Family

Identification:
Dwarf succulent perennials[G] up to 20 cm high. The single, almost egg-shaped stems bear 7–10 radiating 'seams' that alternate with slightly raised, warty[G] ridges. The stem is banded grey-green and striped with dull purple. The leaves are very rudimentary and soon drop off. The flowers are borne in a ring at the top of the stem, and are 3–5 mm in diameter. They are surrounded by five greenish yellow lobes[G] that resemble petals. The sexes are on separate plants.

Succulent type: Stem succulent.

Where found: Hard, stony soil, often under bushes.

Flowering time: March to May.

Notes: One of the most distinctive species of Euphorbia. Has been described as a living baseball with a stitched and chequered cover, and a tartan pincushion. Its curious shape and beautiful colouring has made it a favourite among succulent collectors, leading to destructive collecting of wild specimens. Only a few colonies can be found in the wild, but the plant grows easily from seed and can be bought from specialist suppliers.

Status: Protected. Endemic[G].

Medusa's Head

Euphorbia caput-medusae

Spurge Family

African names:
Vingerpol (Afr)

Identification: Succulent perennials[G] with rosettes of sprawling branches, which arise from a central stem that is largely buried. The branches are 10–30 mm in diameter and are covered with large warts[G]. They ooze a milky sap when damaged. The small, triangular leaves that appear near the branch tips soon drop off. The flowers are carried in small, radiating clusters at the tops of the branches. Flowers are 10–18 mm in diameter and are surrounded by five deeply fringed, green and white lobes[G] that resemble petals.

Succulent type: Stem succulent.

Where found: Sandy coastal flats, but also inland on stony ground.

Flowering time: May to September.

Notes: A favourite among succulent collectors for its very unusual appearance and variable form. It is named after Medusa, one of the three terrifying goddesses of Greek mythology known as the Gorgons. Her head was covered with snakes instead of hair, her hands were of brass, and her body was covered with impregnable scales. The plant's resemblance to Medusa is not difficult to imagine.

Status: Not threatened. Endemic[G].

Yellow Milkbush

Euphorbia mauritanica

Spurge Family

African names:
Geelmelkbos (Afr)

Identification: Many-branched shrubs[G] up to 2 m high with erect, cylindrical branches, 3–6 mm in diameter, that ooze a milky sap when damaged. The small, triangular leaves are in opposite pairs and soon drop off. The flowers are carried in small clusters at the tips of the branches. They are 7–15 mm in diameter and are surrounded by five brilliant, shining yellow lobes[G] that resemble petals.

Succulent type: Stem succulent.

Where found: Sandy coastal flats, but also inland on stony ground.

Flowering time: May to October.

Notes: Reputed to be poisonous and largely avoided by stock, but browsed by steenbok and klipspringer.

Status: Not threatened. Endemic[G].

esser Candelabra Tree

uphorbia cooperi

Spurge Family

African names:
umHlonhlo (Zulu)

Identification: Spiny succulent
trees up to 7 m high, with 4–6
winged branches that are strongly
segmented (like a string of
chunky beads) and that ooze a
milky latex^G when damaged.
There are no leaves. The edges of
the wings are covered with spines
that may run together at the base,
forming a hard rim. The flowers
are crowded along the wing
margins at the tips of the
branches. They are yellowish-
green and 5–7 mm in diameter,
with five fleshy lobes^G that
resemble petals.

Succulent type: Stem succulent.

Where found: Rocky hills in
wooded grassland or scrub^G.

Flowering time: July to
September.

Notes: Resembles the Naboom
but has fewer branches and a
more pronounced segmentation.
The lower side branches die off
regularly to leave a long, naked
bole^G. The milky latex is
extremely poisonous, and can
cause intense irritation and itchi-
ness if it comes in contact with
the skin, and temporary or even
permanent blindness if it comes
in contact with the eyes. Never-
theless, it makes an excellent
garden or container plant,
provided that care is exercised
when moving or trimming it.

Status: Not threatened.

Candelabra Tree

Euphorbia ingens

Spurge Family

African names:
Naboom (Afr),
umHlonhlo,
uMahetheni (Zulu)

Identification: Massive, densely branched succulent trees up to 10 m, with segmented, four-winged branches that ooze a milky latex^G when damaged. There are no leaves, but the edges of the wings may be covered with pairs of spines. The flowers are crowded along the wing margins at the tips of the branches. They are yellowish green, 5–7 mm in diameter, with five fleshy lobes^G that resemble petals.

Succulent type: Stem succulent.

Where found: Widespread in deciduous^G bush or savannah, often on rocky hills or close to termite mounds.

Flowering time: April to June.

Notes: The town of Naboomspruit is this tree's namesake. The milky latex is extremely poisonous, and can cause intense irritation, even permanent blindness. Cattle driven through groves of these trees have been severely burned on the face and eyes. Honey made from the nectar causes a burning in the mouth that is aggravated by drinking water. However, it does make an excellent garden or container plant, provided that care is taken when moving or trimming it.

Status: Not threatened.

Prickly Pear

Opuntia sp

Cactus Family

African names: Turksvy (Afr)

Identification: Densely branched succulent shrubs^G up to 3 m high. They have paddle-shaped or cylindrical stems that are segmented and covered with tufts^G of spines. They do not bear leaves. The flowers vary in colour from yellow and orange to purple, and are scattered along the edges and surfaces of the uppermost segments. The flowers are up to 70 mm in diameter and have numerous petals. The large, fleshy fruits are covered with small, woolly cushions, which bear minute, needle-like bristles.

Succulent type: Stem succulent.

Where found: Throughout southern Africa.

Flowering time: September to December.

Notes: Originally introduced from Central America. Now approximately eleven species of Prickly Pear have been declared weeds throughout South Africa. Several of these have escaped from cultivation^G into the wild and are among the country's most costly invaders. If left unchecked some species can rapidly infest large tracts of land. These areas become inaccessible to man and livestock. Each piece that breaks off the main plant is capable of rooting and establishing a new plant. Because of this all pieces of a plant must be collected and destroyed.

Status: Declared weed.

Glossary

Annual: A plant that completes its lifecycle, from seed germination to flowering and seed production, within a year, and then dies.

Arid: Dry and desert-like.

Basal: At the base, or point of attachment, of a plant's organ.

Biennial: A plant that requires two years to complete its lifecycle, growing vegetatively in the first year, and flowering and fruiting in the second.

Bole: The main trunk of a tree.

Cultivation: The practice of growing plants away from the wild.

Deciduous: Leaves that drop at the end of the growing season, or plants that lose their leaves in this way.

Endemic: Plants that are confined to a particular region.

Epidermis: The outermost layer of cells on a plant, which acts as a skin.

Floret: A small flower, such as those that make up the flowerhead of daisies.

Habitat: The type of place or locality in which a plant grows, such as forest or grassland.

Indigenous: Occurring naturally in a given region or country.

Latex: The milky juice of certain plants, which oozes from wounds.

Lobe: The rounded flap or extension of divided plant organs.

Perennial: A plant that lasts sever years, and does not die after its fir flowering and fruiting season.

Photosynthesis: The process whe carbon dioxide and light are used t form complex carbon compounds needed for plant growth.

Rootstock: An underground stem, usually massive, that sends off bo rootlets and shoots.

Scrub: A type of vegetation, characterised by a cover of stunted trees or shrubs.

Shrub: A woody plant, smaller than a tree, with several main stems from the base instead of a single trunk.

Stamen: One of the male parts of the flower, comprising of an anthe and its filament or stalk.

Stomata: The breathing pores, or apertures, in the epidermis of a plan

Tuber: A very swollen root, or pa of a root.

Tuft: A brush-like bundle or cluste

Twining: Coiling or twisting.

Wart: A small outgrowth or pro-tuberance from the skin of the plan

Whorl: The arrangement of three or more leaves or flowers in a ring around the stem.